Fantastico

By Nicholas Fisk

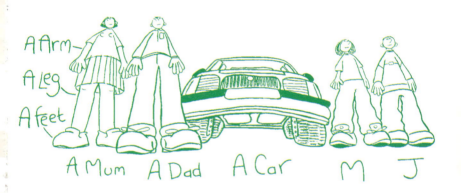

A Arm
A Leg
A feet

A Mum   A Dad   A Car   M   J

Illustrated by Mick Reid

 LONGMAN

Giants

Sending, sending. Are you receiving?

Ah, good. My first report, then.

I had not expected the alien creatures to be so big. Big? They are enormous! Gigantic! And complicated. They move about on jointed limbs, making the ground shake. They are as high as our tallest buildings. When they speak – they are always talking – their bellowings hurt my ears.

Am I afraid of them? I don't think so. I sense nothing threatening or vicious in the mind waves they send out. But what can I know, or you, or any of us?

All we had to go on was the information carried to us by their radio waves. You managed to sort out the fact and fiction in these uncertain, blurred messages. You thought that by studying the broadcasts you would be able to give me a fair enough picture of the creatures I would meet when I arrived here.

How wrong you were!

The *size* of them! The enormous *size!*

Wait: here come two of them. They are entering the cell (sorry – room, they live in rooms) where I am hiding.

Can you hear the thumping noises they make as they move? Can you hear my voice above their noise? I dare not speak any louder ...

M is the smaller of the two but has the most fur on top. It hangs down in waves.

J's fur is darker and the sounds he makes are hoarser. The sounds are talking, the same as we used to listen to on the radio. But sometimes J makes a loud hurr–hurr–hurr noise and once he exploded so violently that the room shook. Then he said, "Pardon. Gotta cold coming." What can that mean?

Their paws are not unlike ours but the fingers are very long and have no fur. At the moment they are using their paws to hold big cans. They put the cans to the holes in their heads, which, like ours, are for talking, drinking, eating and so on.

The cans – they are mugs, that is the right word – hold liquids, definitely. I can hear gurgling sounds as the liquid goes down their food-holes. The mugs are big – I could almost fit into one of them.

J on a chair with a drinking mug

Oh! This is interesting! J has unfolded himself! Now he stands very high and M is still folded and therefore low. Their bodies and limbs must be filled with joints, swivels and pivots. They can extend and retract in all directions. So their bodies are not at all like ours. They must be filled with rods. "Bones?" Did you say "Bones?" Ah, that's the word. Bones, skeletons ... of course. We have nothing like that on our planet.

Oh! Oh! J is coming nearer! Moving on his two enormous platforms! ... You can hear their thundering as they rise and fall, shaking the ground ... Nearer still!

I am not afraid, not afraid, not in the least. I am quite safe if I tuck myself away, hide ... They will never find me here, in this dark corner. All the same, I will close down transmission for now.

Pong

Emma said, "I don't want to watch that crummy old boxing. *Boxing.* Stupid great oiks hitting each other!"

Jason said, "Don't watch it, then. Do your homework. But of course you've already done it! Ha, ha, ha!"

"Listen to who's talking! I suppose you've done yours, like a good little boy?"

"I did most of it on the bus. Some of it, anyhow. Do you want your cocoa?"

"You can have it. I've gone off cocoa, it's a bit yucky."

"Hand it over. Ah, mmm yes, yum yum, goodylicious, slurp slurp. And that thick, rich smell ..."

"You're welcome. Smell ... There's a bit of a pong in this room. A funny pong. Can't you smell it?"

"No. Perhaps you're smelling yourself, ha ha!"

"Ha ha *ha.* And ho ho. No, seriously, can't you smell it?"

"I don't know what you're on about. I'm going to watch the boxing."

No, this world is not at all what you and I expected. So much more complicated.

If only we could have translated their television waves! Then we would have seen what they have got. They use television, of course. J has just left to watch it. Boxing ... What is that? What? I can't hear you very well ... Ah, that's better. Boxing is two men fighting with their paws? Of course. Yes, and football is many creatures fighting with their feet.

Yes, "men." I must stop calling them creatures. There are men and women, right? And boys and girls. What? What? No, I don't know what J and M are. They seem young. One could be a boy and the other a girl but I don't know which is which. You think the one with the longer fur – sorry, hair – is probably the girl. Because girls have longer hair? Oh. I had forgotten that.

What? Say it again ... Yes, I am all right. I will get rid of my food and drink packs, I won't need them. I can find things to eat and I have already drunk liquid – water. It was very good. As soon as I landed I found water everywhere. There were balls of it attached to long green blades growing out of the ground. The blades were almost as high as myself. Some were higher.

Did I try eating the blades? Yes, I did, I knew they must be vegetable matter. Like ours. Grass? I ate grass? Is that what it is? No, it tasted the way it looks ... rich green. Quite nice.

No, don't worry, I quite understand that I must find many sorts of food. That will be no problem. You see, I am inside these creatures' home-place, a great castle made of many materials. And it is filled with foods. Wait ... !

M is putting something in her food-hole right now! She – I will call her 'she', we agree that she is a girl – she is mashing a pale brown solid thing in her food-hole. What a noise it makes! Can you hear? Grunch, grunch, grunch ...

Bits of the crunchy brown thing escape her and fall on the floor. Later I will try eating them, I am sure they will do me no harm.

'Food-hole' is mouth? Mouth, of course. And you think the crunchy round foods could be biscuits? Yes, I suppose they could.

Now she is unfolding herself, rising to her full height. Very tall. She is leaving the room. Can you hear the noise her platforms make? Sorry, feet, shoes on feet. She is leaving, going through the door. Like our doors but more elaborate.

There. Gone. I am alone. Quite alone. No, not afraid. Of course not.

"Em, I think I'll go to bed."

"I thought you were watching the boxing. Crummy boxing."

"Well you were right for once. It was crummy. A fix. You could smell it a mile off."

"I still think there's a weird pong up in that room. A bit like hamsters, but nicer. Do you remember Woofles and Blopples? The poor things ..."

"Old Blopples was all right. *My* hamster. Your Woffles was the disaster. Scabby little ratbag, fur falling out in lumps."

"Blopples was the disaster! You'd never think such a tiny animal could do so many big jobs!"

"Anyway, the hamsters were yonks ago. They're long gone and so is their smell."

"I'm not so sure about that."

False Fur

I am still exploring. Going further afield every day.

In this great house there are six rooms, three on top and three below. And a smaller house for the car. The car – well, we know all about cars from the radio: the sounds they make, what they are for and so on. Cars are very smelly. I do not like to go in the car-house. It makes my fur stink.

Humans are unlucky in one way, they do not have fur except on top. So they wear artificial fur of many sorts – layers of it.

J is definitely a boy, and M a girl. I should have worked that out straight away. Her coverings are different from J's. Both wear tubes over their legs but while J always wears tubes, M sometimes has just a wrapper and her legs show under it. Adults the same.

Their coverings are very important to them. They change them often, I suppose because they are such big, smelly creatures – but also to cheer themselves up.

I am continuing to draw their construction – how they are made, how they work. I am not good at

M
Standing up

drawings and of course I cannot send my drawings
to you now, you are so far away. So far away ...

Sometimes I get lonely, very lonely. But I know
how important my mission is. Now that our
planet is destroying itself, we must find
somewhere to live.

I am the one chosen to explore this world. I
will do my duty, come what may. Depend on that!

But I do get lonely. Do keep talking to me.

"Jay, I thought you said you were going to sleep. That radio of yours ..."

"I didn't say I was going to *sleep,* I said I was going to *bed.* Anyhow, you like rock. You're a real little raver, aren't you? T-shirts, posters, the lot."

"Turn it down or Dad will come up. And I can't do my homework with that *boom, boom, boom* in here, and that pong where I'm working. Really!"

"Still on about the pong? Why?"

"Because ... I don't know ... it's like nothing I've ever smelled before. Not that it matters, I rather like it."

"I've done my homework, all of it. Now that *does* matter. Big deal."

"Come with me and have a sniff round. Switch off the radio. Come on, Jason."

Yoggie Bed

I have made myself a comfortable bed-chamber from bits and pieces left over by the humans. Like us, humans sleep for about a third of their lives. I have taught myself to follow their time-pattern.

I wish you could see me in my bed-chamber! It is basically a container made of 'plastics', not 'china' or 'pottery' or 'glass' (they use so many materials). Anyhow, mine is of plastic, light enough for me to push about. It is called Yoggie.

It still smells of Yoggie, whatever that is. Of course, I clean it every day and the acrid smell is fading.

A Bird made of feathers flying

My bedding is all kinds of stuff – scraps of cloth, paper, feathers from birds, little lengths of wool and cotton to hold things together, and so on. Aired daily.

I like my chamber. I curl my tail over my ears (this is such a noisy world) and have a good sleep. I keep the radio alive of course, hoping that I may hear your voices from out there.

You want to know about birds? They are flying creatures, very clever and very strange. Many shapes and sizes, but always their bodies are covered with feathers (not unlike fur) and their heads finish with a hard, pointed spike. M and J like the birds, particularly M. She saves little pieces of her foods and puts them on a ledge outside the window in this room. The birds fly to the ledge and stab at the food with their spikes.

We have nothing like birds on our planet; no creatures that use the air to walk and run on.

I am lonely, but as you know I keep very busy exploring and recording. My conclusion so far is that this world may prove suitable for us if only because it is so big that our presence would not disturb the humans. They might not even notice us.

I think also that the humans are kind. They do no harm to other creatures. They just get on with their complicated lives.

Oh, pardon – you asked me for a list of people and things in this house. Here it is …

One big male, the Father or Dad. One big female, the Mother or Mum. Then the two children, or kids – the ones I first called J and M, but really their names are Jason and Emma.

There is also a creature called Psss(?). I have not met Psss yet, but I know it exists. I have heard M and J discuss him/her/it. Thus –

"Has Psss shown up?"

"No. Hope he's all right."

You will notice that Psss is referred to as "he" but that does not necessarily mean Psss is a male. The car is sometimes female –

"She took hours to start this morning."

I do not understand this but I do not think it is significant.

Psss

"Jason, look! He's back! Aaah, good old Pussums, come to Emma ... Who's a lovely boy, then?"

"Lovely! You've got to be joking! Just look at him, how manky can you get! Burrs stuck all over his tail. Give him to me, I'll deburr him."

"He's mine, you can't have him. Aaaah, who's a clever cat, then, finding his way home?"

"I want a go, give him to me."

"You can hold him for now while I get him some food. Then I get him back, right?"

"Okay, hand him over. Heh, I think he's lost weight. Where did you go for three whole days? You're a mess, Pussums, aren't you? Hold still ... These burrs ..."

"There, food! Lots of lovely chunkalunks! Right Jason, hand him over."

"He doesn't want *you,* he wants his food. Look at the way he's bolting it down. Pussums the Supernosher."

"That's funny ... Look, Em, why does he keep looking sideways? He keeps staring at the corner cupboard. He's forgotten his food. Hey! Pussums! Chunkalunks!"

"It's no good pushing his nose into the dish like that, how would you like it if –"

"Now what's he doing? What is he after?"

"The corner cupboard, that's what he's after. Just like I was last night. The pong. The smell."

"There isn't any smell."

"Well, Pussums thinks there is. Shall I open the cupboard door for you, Pussums? *There ...*"

"Having a good sniff round, isn't he? Good boy, good boy, sniff it out."

"Oh, he's given up. Gone back to his food. I wonder what all that was about?"

"I'll have a look. Nothing here, Em, just your pile of paperbacks and my dynamo set and some gloves and ... and more gloves ... And an empty Yoggie."

"How disgusting you are, chucking empty food things into the cupboard."

"But I didn't."

"Well, I certainly didn't. Really, Jason –"

"Oh, belt up."

Flesh

My bed-chamber is gone. That is one bad thing. Who took it? Why?

The second bad thing is more serious and alarming. I went to the lower part of this house. I found myself in the kitchen, the room where food is prepared.

On the floor was a blue dish made of plastics. In the dish there was a mound of *flesh*.

Flesh! Oh yes, I recognised it at once. *Flesh*.

This discovery changes everything. Humans eat *flesh*. We do not – could not – eat the bodies of living creatures. Our planet, before it decayed, was full of foods. We had only to pluck what humans would call fruits and vegetables. Never flesh. We would never eat that.

But humans do.

What flesh?

Whose flesh?

Mine?

"Mum was in a rage about your room. Such a mess. Honestly, Jason!"

"She wasn't all that chuffed with yours, remember? Knickers under the bed, tut, tut. Honestly, Emma!"

"Good thing she didn't find your yoghurt pot in the cupboard, ponging away."

"I've told you, it wasn't mine, I didn't leave it there."

"Me neither."

"Well it's gone now, and the pong with it, so who cares?"

"I don't. Bags I the Nintendo. And the pong hasn't gone, at least I don't think so. I'm sure I caught a whiff of it downstairs."

"Forget it. Half an hour on the Nintendo by my watch, then hand over, okay?"

I know now where my bed went. The Mum/Mother can be a very fierce human, she gets into an excited state. She says, "This house is a slum, you live like pigs, out of my way." (Pigs are animal creatures: I do not know what slums are.)

She then cleans the house using various appliances mounted on sticks. Some are furry, some whiskered and one makes a hideous wailing noise as she pushes it back and forth. It hurts my brain.

She cleans everywhere. No doubt she found my bed-chamber and threw it away. I do not mind. I have a new hiding place downstairs. Stairs have steps and where they meet the wall, I found a gap, or hole. I live in this hole and have already made a new bed. I am safe there, the Mum does not come near the hole. I am quite comfortable.

But I am still afraid. These creatures eat *flesh*.

"Can't you smell it, Jay? Here in the cubby-hole? Here under the stairs! Can't you smell it?"

"No. Well, Maybe. But it could be anything."

"But you can smell it?"

"No ... yes ... It's not a bad smell."

"Pussums was sniffing about in here, this morning. But then he went away."

"Bored rotten, I suppose. Like me. Shall I tell you what you can do with your smell? Shall I?"

"If you do, I'll tell Dad."

Monster

There is a monster in this house, a very terrible one.

It is the creature I called Psss. I was trying to say the real name, Pussums. It is black all over except for the eyes, which are a glaring yellow, so bright that they seem to be lit from inside. It is four or five times my size, and armed with hideous fangs.

Fangs that could tear flesh.

I admit I am terrified of this creature. Not because it is so big. Not because of its quick, smooth, silent, deadly way of moving. But because I sense, I *feel,* that it is made to hunt and kill ...

To kill what? Who? Perhaps *me.*

Listen! Can you hear this? Or is it too faint? That "Fff ... fff!" sound comes from the creature's nose. It is sniffing at the entrance to my hiding place!

And there! - surely you heard that! It talked! Did you hear the word? Here it is again ...

"Mu. Mu."

It is asking questions, I think. Asking,

"What is this hidden thing? How can I get to it?"

"Mu-mu-mu ... Snif ... mu ... sniff ..."

Thank the stars! It has gone away and my heart is no longer thundering.

Oh come on now, be brave, be sensible, put your brain to work.

Very well. Pussums is a creature of the same order as Jay and Em. Heart, lungs, food in/out system, etc. Like Jay and Em, it is constructed of a layer of flesh stretched over jointed bones.

A Psss

So these creatures are different from us. We do not need bones inside our bodies. We have structures of varying hardness and elasticity. Of course you know all this, everyone does, but I find it calming to talk of such things.

Suppose Pussums managed to get in here and attack me! But it couldn't, its body is too big. Suppose it attacked me when I was out in the open! I cannot spend all my time hidden, I must go out and explore if I am to be of value. Suppose Pussums tracked me down, sprang at me, bit me with its fangs! No, I am cleverer than it. I could defend myself. I must think how. Think hard. Concentrate ...

"All over, Em! For the time being, anyway. No more school, no more homework, for days and days! Away-break, here we come!"

"Half term, half term – and about time too! 'No more Latin, No more Greek, No more cane to make me squeak'. I read that in one of Granpa's old comics. Or perhaps it was Dad's."

"'No more cane to make me squeak'... Dad was never caned at school, was he?"

"It's a pity they dropped caning – for boys. If you were caned, Jason, you'd be greatly improved. Caned every hour on the hour, on your scrawny bottom."

"Who's got skinny arms? Whose ears stick out?"

"It's half term, let's not quarrel –"

"Who started it? You did. But anyhow ... Latin and Greek. They really did teach that, I wonder why?"

"I wonder why we don't all speak the same language. And I wonder what language Pussums speaks."

"Oh, just miaow and brrps and purr."

"Poor old Pussums, I'll miss him when we're on our away-break. I don't suppose he will miss us. But he knows something is up. He keeps sniffing at the suitcases. Are you sure you have packed everything?"

"All packed up and ready to go. Look at them, our suitcases! What a beautiful sight! We're going away, on holiday!"

"I suppose we'd better take them downstairs. Stack them in the cubby-hole under the stairs."

Trapped

I'm locked in! Trapped!

I heard footsteps, then a great crash. Everything went dark. Well, almost dark. There was a chink of light left. Then there were more footsteps and another great crash and some huge thing was thrust against the first thing and now it is completely dark.

What? What? Yes, I am receiving you ... Yes, I will try and explain more clearly. I am in my hiding place, the hole in the wall where the staircase meets it. A solid thing has been placed where it blocks my hole. And then another thing.

So I am trapped. No, I am not panicking. Yes, I will try and find out what the things are that block my hiding place.

I feel a hard, slippery surface. Like a wall. I cannot move it.

No, wait: if I press with all my strength, there is some movement, the wall gives a little. But only a little.

What did you say? Could I find something to

drill through it? That's ridiculous, *what* thing? It is all right for you, you are not trapped in a dark place ...

Wait! Of course, here it is, I am holding it, it was here all the time. A long, strong spear of metal, cut in a spiral, slotted across the head – and with a very sharp point.

Yes, I think I can drill with it, or scrape with it, or do *something.* No, it is not too heavy. It is about half my height. I can hold it with both paws, then lean forward with all my weight ... like this ... and ...yes ... I am making some impression ... But it is very tiring ...

Now start again.

Very well, then. Push. Twist. Push. Harder. *Harder.*

I think I am succeeding. I *must* succeed.

My escape thing

Apeman

"Apeman Andy's here. Where can we hide, Em?"

"He shouldn't be here, it's not his mum's day to help out. And it's no good hiding, you know that. He always find us. Or Mum digs us out to be nice to him."

"Mum's not in, she's picking up the tickets at the travel agent's. We *could* hide."

"You know what Mum says, Jason. 'You've got to be kind to Andy, he's had a terrible life. It's your duty to help him relate; to *find* himself.'"

"I don't mind him finding himself, I just don't want him to find me."

"But Mum says –"

"Look, he's walking up and down the garden. And he's got a stick. Bet you anything you like he knocks the heads off the flowers."

"Mum says he's underprivileged, a social misfit. The awful things he does are a cry for help."

"There you are, told you so, he's bashing the hedge. And doing his mouthing bit. He's going 'Grrr, yah, ged-out-of-it!'"

"Oh dear, I suppose we've got to go out there. *You* go, Jason."

"Oh no! Ladies first. *You* do it."

"You're the macho male. Don't tell me you're afraid?"

"Sure I'm afraid. Andy is a murderous moron."

"He's not. He's just a bit ...weird."

"Look, Em, now he's picking up stones! He's chucking them! He'll hit Pussums!"

"No he wont. He likes Pussums and Pussums likes him."

"Then Pussums is a moron too."

It's no good. I've worked and worked, but I am only scratching at the solid wall keeping me prisoner. I am exhausted. It is all so hopeless, I managed to make a hole with the tool I am using – but it's too small, it's no good. I'll never get free.

I cannot go on. Perhaps I will die here. Stupidly. Miserably. Pointlessly.

I have let you all down. What an ending to the great voyage of exploration!

"Oh dear! Oh dear! Pardon the intrusion, Jason – so sorry Emma, I know it's not one of my days –

but I've got to find that son of mine, my Andy. Andy, *Andy!* Come when your mother calls! Come on, now!"

"Coming, Mum." (Under his breath: "Grrr! Yah!")

"Well, look sharp about it! And put that stick down, you don't need no stick."

"I've put it down, Mum." (Under his breath: "Silly old moo!")

"I mean, really, making me traipse all this way to find him! He knows he's not supposed to be here without me. And I'll be over in the next day or two anyhow. Your Mum's asked me to pop in and water the house plants ... You're all packed up and ready to go, right? Well, now, isn't that exciting. Where are the bags? In the hall? Well, Andy can make himself useful for once. Go and fetch them, Andy. Carry them out. Well go on, stir your stumps!"

"Yes, Mum." (Under his breath: "Old moo, old stupid, I hate you!")

"And don't bang things about, you be careful. Well, that will keep him out of mischief for a moment or two ... Yes, put them in the garage, Andy. No, not like that, they'll get run over. Put them neatly to one side against the wall."

"Like this, Mum?" (Under his breath: "Old moo. Moo, moo, moo!")

"Yes, like that. Then they can go straight in the boot. Right then. We'll be off. Come on, Andy! Come *on!*"

A miracle! I am free! The great wall blocking my hiding place is gone!

I don't know where, or how, or why. All I know is, that there were human footsteps, and a muttering human voice; and then part of the wall seemed to be carried away – and then *my* part of it, the part I had been trying to drill through.

The footsteps went away. I still heard muttering and grumbling noises, but I paid no attention. Air and light streamed in – the way is clear! I am free!

I will move out at once. Never mind the risks. Never mind the big black furry creature. I must go outside, see the sky, smell the air...

I'm free!

"Thank goodness they're gone, Em. I can't stand them. Andy, Andy's mum ..."

"She's worse, in a way. That dyed hair, and all that crooked lipstick. And that look in her eye."

A tree

A House

A Car house

"She's got a sort of ... murderer's look. Like she'd go for you with a red-hot corkscrew or something. *Torture* you. Horror-movie stuff."

"Poor Andy, he's just a weirdo. But *she* ... I don't know. And anyhow, where's his dad?"

"In the slammer, I suppose. Life imprisonment for carrying out the murders she plans."

"Well, they're gone now, and we'll be gone tomorrow. Can't wait."

"What was that?"

"What was what?"

"I thought I saw something moving – moving fast – an animal or something. It disappeared in that bush."

"Pussums."

"It wasn't Pussums, it was the wrong colour. Colours. Several colours."

"A hedgehog."

"No ... but that sort of thing."

"You frightened yourself with all that stuff about murderers."

"Maybe that was it. Listen, is that Mum in the car? Yes it is, I'll load the suitcases into the boot."

Away-break

"Goodbye Pussums, goodbye! Ah, poor Pussums, don't cry, we'll be back soon."

"He's not crying, he's yawning. He's had enough of your slop."

"Next-door's putting your food out, Pussums, you won't be left all alone."

"*You'll* be left all alone if you don't get moving. Dad's blowing the horn again."

"Oh, poor Pussums, try not to miss me too much and don't forget to eat your food, you mustn't starve with grief."

"Fat chance. Got a belly like a football, haven't you, Pussums? All fat and furry ..."

"Dad's blowing the horn again. Come *on*, Jason."

It is wonderful to be outside again. Trees, sky, air, flowers, little things that fly on lace wings, big birds. Such a wonderful planet! I do hope we can settle in this miraculous, rich world! How many different creatures are there in it, I wonder? How many sorts of living things?

Living things ... but humans kill them to eat their flesh. I have found out all about it.

There goes a bird ... even it is eating flesh: a pale wriggly thing. It has pulled it out of the earth. Now it is eating it.

Flesh, they all eat flesh, Pussums, birds, humans, everyone. And we are small and made of flesh.

Ouch!

That was close. Too close.

Pussums – the creature I called Psss, the cat – saw me. Saw me and followed me. But I am safe. I have a special outdoor hiding place. He cannot get into it. But I can.

Lord of All

I am Me. The Lord of All. Cat.

I am master. I own everything. This grass is mine to roll in. This earth is mine to scratch after I have blessed it with personal offerings. That house is mine and all the soft places in it. The big animals within the house obey my commands: let me in, let me out, caress me, give me food and drink. All must obey me –

What was that?

All night, I prowl, I pounce, I kill. All day, I lick my beautiful fur, I sleep, I –

Something moved – a creature, an animal.

I own everything except the sky. I do not want the sky, only the flying animals that use it. I crouch, I quiver, I pounce –

It is gone, but its smell remains. A new smell, unknown to me.

Slowly now ... carefully ... silently ... Follow the smell ... so carefully, so silently.

Curses! Damnation! That boy from another place has returned and I must give up the chase!

Kickstone

"Left it here somewhere, I did, my favourite kick-stone. Mum won't let me kick cans 'cos of the racket but she can't stop me kicking my kick-stone along the road. Give it another kick, it skids along the pavement, falls in the gutter, tries to hide. But I always find it. But now I've lost it. My kick-stone, where are you?

"It's here somewhere. Fell out of my pocket. Pocket with the hole in it. Catch Mum mending my pocket, doing anything for me. She hates me, I hate her. Moo, old moo.

"And Jason, Emma, I hate them too. Stuck-up grotbags, think they're so smart and clever – couple of nerds. Call me Apeman Andy they do. Oh I know all about it, they think I'm a dumbo but I could show them a thing or two.

"Not just now, though. I'm safe. It's raining, Mum won't come out in the rain, might get her grotty hair wet, all that dye running down, I'd laugh. No she won't come and get at me now, get at me properly, the way she does.

"Nor Dad. Dad! I'll get you one day, Dad, see if I don't. Give you a dose of what you give me. Thumps.

"Ah! There you are! My stone, my kick-stone. Thought you'd get away from me, didn't you, but here you are, my best friend, my pal. My only pal.

"Oh, and there's Pussums. *They've* got a cat, got everything. No cat for *us,* natch. Wish I had a cat. One for myself. A tabby, not black like Pussums. But Pussums is all right. But he shouldn't run away from me like that, that's rude. Chuck a stone near him, wake him up, make him mind his manners. Watch out, Pussums!"

Mrrraow!

Pussums ran after me. He smelled me, followed my scent. I ran away from him as fast as my short legs could carry me. I went straight to my special outdoor hiding place, under a bush.

There are things called shrubs and bushes, like little trees. Under my particular bush there is a green container made of plastics. It has a hole in the top to let the water in and a spout to let it out; and a carrying handle. It was left in my hiding place under my bush. This container suits me perfectly: I can get into the hole but Pussums cannot, the hole is too small. So I ran and ran,

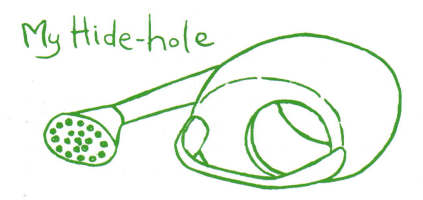

My Hide-hole

knowing I would be safe if only I got there in time.

But the container was gone! Gone! And the black monster bounding towards me! ...

I turned to face it. It stopped running and crouched, with its chin touching the ground and its shoulders raised like two black hills. A hideous noise came from its throat

MRRRR-AOW! MRRRK ... MEW-AOW!

A relishing growl, a final threat before the spring; a sound that meant, "I have you now, I will kill you soon!"

That was when the boy – I had not even noticed his presence – threw the stone. He threw it hard. It whizzed.

The whizz ended in a dull thump – and the cat screeched – leaped in the air, spinning above me – and thumped down on the wet earth.

It did not move, it just lay there. Soon, raindrops made a silvery dew over its black fur.

I had been out of my mind with fear. Now the fear was replaced by awe, and pity. My enemy was no longer a dreadful monster. Now the pink mouth was open and snarling but the white fangs would not hurt me. The row of small teeth between the fangs were as pretty and innocent as a string of beads.

Then the boy loomed above me. He gaped. Wide-eyed, staring down at the cat, he muttered:

"But ... but ... I didn't mean..."

Stupid Stone

"I didn't mean to hurt you, Pussums honest I didn't, I'm always chucking stones, I never thought I'd hit you. I didn't mean it.

"Oh gawd, I wish it hadn't hit you, that stupid stone. You're all right you are, not like people. I'd never hurt you. That stupid stone ... You're not dead, you're just pretending, aren't you?

"Jason, Emma, and their Mum and Dad, they're real nerkers, make you sick. And *my* Mum and Dad, I'd kill them if I could, give it to them real good the way they do it to me. Her pinching and slapping and chucking me out of the house and him knocking me about, smashing at me with his big hard fists. And her yelling "Don't hit him in the face where it will notice, not in the face!"

"One day I'll fix 'em, just wait.

"But you ... poor old moggy, you like it when I tickle your chin, don't you? And stroke you and all. You go 'Purr, purr.' We have real talks. I tell you things I never tell anyone else.

"And now that stupid stone has bashed you, if

only it had missed. I didn't mean it, I never thought to hurt you, honest."

The cat moved! I was so amazed that I forgot about hiding.

The cat's legs twitched and jerked. It tried to raise its head. It moved! It lived!

Then the strangest thing happened. It spoke. It did not merely make a sound, it spoke in my language, using our words. It said, "Be kind. I hurt."

It did not speak our language well. But the sound was right – it spoke on our high notes, not on the low pitch of humans that I cannot manage.

I could not mistake the meaning of its words. I said,

"I will help you. I promise I will."

The cat said, "Please. I hurt."

The boy said nothing. He just stood there, gaping. Wet stuff was coming out of his eyes.

Then he saw me – and gave a cry of amazement.

Blue Tabby?

"Pussums and this weird little animal – they were talking to each other, they really were. I thought I'd killed Pussums but I hadn't, he was alive. And talking to this animal.

"First Pussums said 'Mew' – real feeble, right up high. 'Mew, mew,' he went.

"This other animal there, you'd never believe such a thing! About the size of a hedgehog and that sort of shape, bunchy, with little legs and big bright eyes. I thought I was dreaming. There's no such animal, but there was and it was there, with fur like, you know, nylon. Fine and shiny and silky.

"And colours! A dark line running down from its forehead to its little tail. Real tiny tail. Then bands of lighter colours, stripes and bands, like a tabby. No, not like a tabby. I mean, who's ever seen blue on a tabby?

"Blue like a peacock's blue and catching the light and all. More like feathers than fur. And all those brilliant colours, bands of them. Fantastic, unbelievable.

"You'd never believe me neither when I tell you it spoke. Cat-language, that is what it spoke. High sounds like mewing. No, wait, it was the cat spoke first, it gave a couple of mews, then this weirdo animal made the same sounds but different because it was answering, telling Pussums something.

"The rain was falling, Pussums was all draggled and so was this other animal. It didn't like that, it gave little shakes and the water flew off. And it kept licking itself, preening. Vain. Proud of its feathers, or fur or what-you-call-it.

"So Pussums and the other animal were talking back and forth. And Pussums tried to get up but the other one said 'No.' I could tell it said that, and Pussums lay back and the other one moved up alongside Pussums and started doing things with its tongue or mouth to the place where that stupid stone hit Pussums.

"Pussums got better. Quite quickly. The other one used its paws and all, making Pussums better. Paws with fingers, you can just see them under the fur and feather. Proper little hands, real clever.

"The rain stopped. Pussums started purring – and you know what? The other one tried to purr too. It couldn't do it well, but it tried. You'd have laughed.

"I wasn't laughing, I was just glad. I like killing wasps, and carrion crows if I can get a stone near them (which I can't). I like chucking stones at things and hitting stupid flowers with sticks. No flowers in our house and no flowers in the garden neither, just bits of motors and washing machines and that. Flowers! You must be joking. Yes, I like smashing and bashing, the way Mum and Dad smash and bash me. Get my own back.

"But Pussums – you wouldn't do him no harm, you tickle him around his ears to make him purr. That's what this other animal ended up doing. I think he'd cured Pussums and now he was trying to make him feel good.

"I stroked Pussums too and he purred some more."

"Home again, home again, jiggety-jig. I didn't like leaving our holiday home, did you, Em?"

"No, but it's good to be home. Look! – just a few days gone, and the grass needs cutting! Get the mower going, Jason!"

"You get it going. I want something to drink. A fruit juice from the fridge."

"I'll talk to Andy, give him his present. It was nice of him to welcome us home."

"He didn't welcome us, he just stood there gawping."

"He was welcoming us just by being there."

"I'll go to the kitchen and get a drink."

So Sleepy

The family is back! I missed them more than I thought I would.

Pussums stood by the car. He rubbed against their legs as they got out, yet he says he does not care about them.

Andy was there too. He is the boy who threw the stone. He is not a bad boy. In fact, he is very good to me and Pussums.

Pussums is sleeping now. No he is not, he is yawning. Yawning, yawning ... That is one thing we have in common, these Earth creatures and myself. Yawning is catching, it makes you sleepy. I am sleepy, so sleepy, I have been asleep and I want to go back to sleep. I mustn't of course, I must hide away because the family is back.

But it is so warm on this kitchen rug, curled up against Pussums. So sleepy ...

Pinch Me!

"Em! Quickly! Come with me! Don't make a sound! You won't believe it!"

"Believe what? Andy has been telling me about an animal with crazy-coloured fur. You're right, he's barmy –"

"Never mind that. Come with me. Keep quiet. Not a sound."

"I gave Andy his present, at first he looked sort of baffled –"

"Be quiet. Just follow me. In the kitchen, they're there."

"Dad wants you to help with the bags –"

"Sssh! There. *There!* Take a good look!"

"Jason, oh Jason! It's impossible! I'm dreaming!"

"Look at its tummy going up and down. It's breathing, like Pussums. It's *real.*"

"I still don't believe it! Pinch me, Jay. No stop, that hurts. I do believe it. It's real."

"Unbelievable. Fantastico."

"I told Em, but she wouldn't believe me. About Pussum's friend I mean, this other creature. Then she gave me this present, it's great. Really nice of her. She and her brother, they're all right really. Giving me a present and all, that's real nice.

"A little radio she gave me. From both of them. Listen, it works a treat! Mains or battery. A real surprise.

"And aren't *they* in for a surprise when they see *it!*'

"Look, Em, Pussums is waking up. Hello Pussums! Good Pussums! There ... there ... We're back."

"Pussums, who's your beautiful friend?"

"Fantastico, that's who he is. We'll call him Fantastico."

"That fur, those colours! Should we wake him? What shall we do about him?"

"I just don't know. I'm trying to work things out. He must have been here a long time, always hiding."

"How do you know that?"

"The smell. The mystery smell. It was him. Can't you smell it? Of course you can."

"You're right. The smell ... even that's fantastico. What do we do about him? Do we show him to Mum and Dad?"

"I don't think so. No. Because they'd make it all complicated, the way grown-ups do. Let's just wait for him to wake up and see what he does."

I woke up and there they were, kneeling on the kitchen rug, looking down at me. They stared and stared, then they touched me the way they do Pussums. Stroking.

I was terrified. I asked Pussums a simple question
– "?" – and he answered,

"Oh, them. They are all right."

The two of them, Jason and Emma, stayed with
me a long time, admiring me, stroking me and
saying how beautiful my eyes are. And my fur.
They kept asking each other, "What shall we do
with him?"

I showed them what to do. I gave a great yawn
and curled up again inside the curve of Pussums'
warm body. I was half asleep when they picked
me up and carried me away.

"Fantastico, Fantastico … I can't get over him. But
what will we do?"

"Just leave it all to him. He'll be all right. He'll
know what to do now we've hidden him in your
bedroom."

"He was all drowsy when I carried him
upstairs. Pussums followed me up. They're both
asleep again by now, I bet."

"Leave it at that, Em. Pussums looks great. Did
Andy like his present?"

"He just took it and switched it on and said
'You shouldn't have, you shouldn't have'. He

wouldn't look at me, he held his head down and fumbled with the radio. I think he was, what's the word, overcome."

"Not used to getting presents. Good old Andy, he certainly looked after Pussums."

"And Fantastico."

Heinz Home

Life is great. I am very happy.

Emma and Jason have constructed a beautiful home for me. It is called Heinz 57. The doors flap open or shut and I have a proper bed made of shirts. The shirts are changed regularly after they have been washed.

I have many kinds of food – Emma and Jason say I must try everything, and everything is new and interesting. Of course I never eat anything that smells of flesh.

I also have special bowls for drinks such as water, orange juice, milk and cocoa. Cocoa is Emma's favourite. I do not like it very much but I drink it because she likes to see me pretend to enjoy it. She watches and smiles. That is another thing we have in common with Earth people: smiling.

I never see the Mum or Dad. I am kept hidden from them. I do not know or care about the reason. But Andy visits me often.

It was through Andy that I made my great discovery – *music*. I never understood about music until Andy played his radio to me. Oh, I knew – all of us did – about those strange up-and-down wailing noises that came through to us on the radio waves: but we always thought they were just interference, didn't we? So we tuned them out.

But it was music! I suddenly understood this when Andy echoed the music sounds from the

A Radio

radio. He joined in. And then I knew: the noises were controlled, they had meanings, they were *music*.

I shall always remember the moment when I understood – I will never forget the song. It was called 'Eleanor Rigby'. The radio sang it, Andy sang it ... and so did I.

Music is easy. Anyone can do it. Emma and Jason do it often. But when I joined in that first time, they were amazed! They made me learn to sing many tunes. I can do tunes straight away, I only have to hear them – 'God Save the Queen', 'Pop Goes the Weasel', any tune at all.

They like to hear me sing. They say my voice is like a tiny violin or like air escaping from a balloon. Obviously I have a very fine voice.

Sing Talk

"Fantasico is – well, fantastic, isn't he? Using music and tunes the way he does. To talk to us! Don't you think he's brill, Em?"

"Of course he is. And he's getting better all the time. I gave him coffee for the first time this morning, and he didn't like it, so he started singing 'Cool, Clear Water'."

"And at his bedtime last night, he sang that song which goes 'Goodnight, my love, sleep tight, my love'."

"He loves talking to us like that. He smiles all the time he's singing."

"No he doesn't. Em, don't you remember? He wasn't smiling when he held my finger and sang 'Over There, Over There'. And what was the other one? Yes, I remember: 'Off We Go into the Wild Blue Yonder'. He wasn't smiling then. Just staring with those great shiny eyes. All solemn."

"You're imagining it. He was just sleepy."

"Maybe. But why did he keep waving his paw? Waving it like this ... little short flaps of his hand? He was trying to tell us something serious."

Oh please let them understand! Please make their brains work out what I was trying to tell them!

I'm going, leaving, quitting Earth. Not because I want to but because I must. Orders are orders. I am ordered home.

I want to go home, of course I do. But I do not want to leave Emma, Jason, Andy and Pussums. They have become part of me and I of them. I feel the rays coming from their minds. Warm. Kind.

Very soon now. Tonight. The ship will come, the beam will descend. It will find me, cradle me, carry me up. So I must leave them. Never see them again. Never talk to them again, even. Unless they understand what I tried to tell them.

They must understand.

Sky Light

I am Cat, Lord of All. Nothing can hurt or disturb me.

Then why do I feel disturbed? Even hurt? He simply went. He never said goodbye.

There was a noise in the night, a wrong noise. The humans did not hear it but I did. Because I am Cat. I went through my flap, entered the garden saw the light in the sky. The light moved. A beam came down. The noise became louder – LOUDER – then faded and was gone.

And *he* was gone.

Now I must lie on the rug all alone, without my friend curled up against me, purring as I purr and speaking almost as I speak.

Alone. But of course I do not care, because I am Cat ...

"He's gone. Gone for ever. I wish I were dead."

"So do I when you keep snivelling. Oh, come on, Em! It's not the end of the world! He was only –"

"Only the most gorgeous thing there ever was. Fantastico, why did you leave us? Why?"

"He got sick of your moaning and groaning, likely. Come *on,* Em! We're supposed to be thinking – working out what he meant! *Think!"*

"I don't want to think, Jason. Just curl up and die."

"Listen, Em. We agree that the songs he sang were all about leaving, right? The 'Wild Blue Yonder' and all that. Agreed?"

"All right, agreed. But the other business – when he held on to you and waved his paw in little jerks – what was that supposed to mean?"

"That was the important bit, for heaven's sake! The bit we haven't solved! Wave, wave ... little waves ..."

"JASON! I'VE GOT IT!"

Always ... Always

"I've got him, I'm sure I have! On my little radio. I've been trying for hours, I was nearly asleep just then, with the radio squeaking and whistling. On short waves, of course. Like Fantastico told us. Clever of him that was.

"Ah, here he is again. He's cutting through all that foreign muck. He can't do it very often, but he's getting through now ...'

"'I'll be seeing you ... In everything that's light and gay ...'"

"Go on, Fantastico! Do some more! Prove it's really you!"

"'We'll meet again, don't know where, don't know when ...'"

"Good thing I know all those crummy old songs. Good thing he can sing them in that squeaky old voice of his!"

"'But I know we'll meet again some sunny day!'"

"Ah! He keeps singing that line! Listen to him now!"

"'I KNOW we'll meet again... I KNOW we'll meet again! ...'"

"Can't be more definite than that, can he? And now he'll sign off, like he always does. Yes, here it comes, told you so ..."

"'I'll be loving you, always ... always ... always ...'"

"So he's coming back. For sure. 'Some day soon', he sang that. And 'Roll on harvest moon', he did that one too. Harvest is autumn. He'll be here in autumn.

"Will he bring his chums? Hope he does. Roll on autumn! Welcome home, Fantastico!"